How to Make Wine

The Essential Guide
to Making Wine at Home

by Gabriella Vintoni

Table of Contents

Introduction

Whether you're a wine connoisseur or just someone who enjoys the occasional glass of wine, nothing tastes better than the wine you create yourself. Making wine at home really isn't as complicated as it seems, and in fact it doesn't cost a fortune either.

How fantastic would it be to have your friends over for dinner and impress them with your homemade wine? Or even to come home at the end of a long work day and relax on the porch with a glass of wine made all by yourself?

This book was written to provide you with step-by-step instructions to walk you through the entire process of making your own wine, from start to finish. From preparing the fruit, to perfecting the fermentation process, and to bottling, this book's got it covered. Also included also are delicious, tried and true recipes for several variations of both red and white wine that you can use to develop and hone your winemaking skills.

So if you share a passion for wine and are ready to try your hand at making your own to impress and share with your friends and family, then download this book and let's get started!

Chapter 1: Getting to Know the Ingredients

This chapter will give you some general notes on the ingredients you will need to make wine.

1. Juice

Believe it or not, for making wine, you can choose almost any fruit that has lots of juice. You don't even necessarily have to use grapes, although they work great and will taste the most like traditional bottled wine.

If you don't have fresh fruit, you can buy juice as well but always check the label to make sure that the juice does not contain any additives. Only vitamin C or ascorbic acid is allowed. If you use fresh fruit, you will have to juice it first. As for the amount, if you want to make 5 gallons of wine, you will need 5 gallons of juice.

2. Sugar

Sugar is important because it helps the yeast grow. Also, the amount of sugar you use, as well as the type of sugar, will determine the flavor of your wine and the percentage of alcohol. Corn sugar or dextrose is typically used, but you can experiment with other types of sugar as well, such as brown or white sugar. For 5 gallons of wine, you will need about 4 pounds of sugar.

3. Yeast

There are many types of champagne or wine yeast and they all work fine. However, if you don't have any wine yeast and think that baker's yeast can be used as a substitute, you're wrong. Baker's yeast leaves a specific taste to the products it is added to. Moreover, when added to the must (the solution of sugar, water, fruit pulp and fruit juice), its action is visible only to the upper levels of the must; and when the alcohol develops in the must, it kills the baker's yeast. All of this is avoided with wine yeast. Also, do not use high-alcohol or distiller's yeast because you will get very bad wine. As for the amount, one packet is usually enough for 5 gallons.

Why is yeast so important? When you add the yeast to the must, it rapidly reproduces and the byproduct of this reproduction is carbon dioxide. Carbon dioxide removes oxygen from the must, which allows the yeast to start consuming the sugar and thus produce alcohol. Your must is converted to wine when the yeast consumes all the sugar.

4. Chemicals

Chemicals are used in small amounts and if you use them properly, they will not change the flavor of your wine. They can be found at home brew or chemical supply stores. Some of the chemicals you may use include:

Sodium/Potassium Metabisulfite. It allows the yeast to grow and preserves the wine. You will use this if you use fresh fruit; but in case you have decided to buy juice, you will not need this one. Also, if you are allergic to sulfites, do not use this.

Potassium Sorbate. If you want to add more sugar to your wine but don't want to activate the yeast again, you can use this chemical which will allow you do exactly that—add sugar without activating the yeast.

Yeast nutrient. This one is not necessary but is recommended because it helps the yeast work faster and there are also fewer chances that the wine will get an off-taste.

When using chemicals, double-check the label and follow the instructions on the package so that you know what amount of the chemical to use for the amount of juice.

Chapter 2: Acquiring the Equipment

This chapter will give you a list of equipment you will need for making wine at home. These things can be bought either at home brew stores or online. If you buy online, you may get discounts on certain items, such as the hydrometer or siphon tube.

1. Container—glass jug or plastic bottle

It is important that the container you use is either made of glass or food-grade plastic. Any other material will not work; if you use anything else, during the process of fermentation, your wine may oxidize, which will result in the wine having a stale taste. If you use a glass jug, check on the inside to make sure that there are no scratches. Crockery and wood are not ideal materials for this container because they cannot be completely cleaned. Moreover, make sure that your container is large, or that it holds at least eight gallons. Smaller containers are not suitable because the fermentation process is vigorous so liquid may spill out if the container is small.

2. Small mesh sack

This sack will be left in the main container during fermentation and will be filled with fruit pulp. It should be made of porous material.

3. Airlock

Airlocks serve to let the gas produced by the yeast out and to prevent outside air from entering the container. For this purpose, you can use a balloon, a commercial airlock or plastic wrap and rubber bands.

A balloon. If you use a balloon, attach it to the container with some rubber bands. The yeast will release CO_2, which will cause the balloon to expand. When inflated to a certain point, the CO_2 will start to escape, but since the pressure inside the balloon is greater than the pressure outside, air is not allowed in.

Airlock. You can also buy an airlock. It consists of three parts and it usually goes with some alcohol, which serves to submerge the center pipe or the bigger part. If you use this kind of airlock, you will need to get a rubber stopper as well. When buying a rubber stopper, take #8 or #9. These should work and you should also make a ¼ hole in this rubber stop. In case you use a commercial airlock, you can follow the instructions on the package, but generally you will need to stick the airlock into the rubber stopper and then stick this assembly into the neck of the container. You will need to fill the bigger piece of your airlock with some alcoholic drink, and then place the smaller part on top of it. Finally, close the airlock with its lead or top. The price of airlocks varies from about $5 to $7, and they can be found at wine supply shops.

Rubber bands and plastic wrap. If using rubber bands and plastic wrap, you can place a piece of plastic wrap over the mouth of the gallon jug and then use a rubber band to secure it. This will serve as your trap or airlock. You should make sure not to stretch the plastic wrap too tightly because as the pressure rises in the container, the plastic wrap will stretch to let the gas from the inside out and if it is too tight, it may rupture.

4. Stirrer

This serves to mix your solution. The best option is to use a long plastic handle or stick. You can use a wooden handle as well.

5. Funnel

This is a simple funnel that you will use when pouring liquid into the container.

6. Siphon

A siphon is a flexible clear plastic or rubber tubing. It is used to transfer the liquid from the container into the jugs or bottles. This is an important piece of equipment. If the wine is exposed to air, oxygen can react with an undeveloped wine and cause the wine to have a nutty flavor. It's important that it is super clean and hasn't been used for siphoning something else which can give your wine an off-taste. You can get a siphon for around $4 at any home brew store or online.

7. One-gallon small-mouth jugs

These will be used for secondary fermentation, and may be either plastic or glass. Colored glass works fine as well, but clear glass jugs are preferable because you will have to check on the wine during the secondary fermentation.

8. Hydrometer

This is a device that measures liquid density. Once you buy your hydrometer, you will get complete instructions with the package. When making your own wine, you will use a hydrometer to tell you how much sugar to add to produce the percentage of alcohol you want. Also, remember that temperature causes changes in the density of liquids. So, check the specific gravity of your wine only at a specific temperature if you want it to be accurate. You will need to spend up to $17 for a hydrometer that will serve your purposes. Hydrometers can be found either at home brew or wine supply stores, or online. If you want to spend less money on this piece of equipment, then it's better to search the Internet and try to look for discounts.

9. Bottles

These will be used for storing the finished product. You can use jugs or 2l bottles. Make sure to clean the bottles well and tighten the tops. You can use bottles that are closed with screw caps or plastic corks. The thing with plastic corks is that they can only be used for a few times because they may become worn and thus lose their ability to seal the bottle properly.

10. Sanitizer

This is a very important part of the equipment, as you will need to clean all the equipment thoroughly. If not, your wine will taste like vinegar. Several things can be used as a sanitizer.

If you want to buy something cheap, you can use **bleach** but you should know that this is not the option if you want good wine. The downside of this is that you will be left with a chemical smell unless you rinse it thoroughly.

Iodine sanitizing solution can be used as well. It can be easily found and is not very expensive.

The best option is to use **Star-San sanitizer** or **B-T-F Iodophor**. You just need to follow the package instructions. These can be obtained at homebrew stores.

Chapter 3:   The   Step-by-Step Procedure of Wine-Making

Depending on type of wine, some steps of the wine making process may differ; but I will present you with some general steps which you may follow.

Step 1: Wash the fruit

Rinse the fruit you are going to use thoroughly, especially if it's non-organic or has been sprayed with fertilizer.

Step 2: Get the juice

Crush the grapes, berries or anything you decided to use, in order to get the juice out. There are different ways to do this. You can use a press to crush the fruit, or do it by hand.

Step 3: Collect the pulp

Fill a nylon sack with the crushed fruit, hold it over a can and squeeze gently to release the juice from the pulp. Repeat until all the fruit has been squeezed and the pulp is in the sack. Close the sack and leave it in the container with the juice.

Step 4: Vitamin C

Add the vitamin C or ascorbic acid. This will keep the wine from oxidizing and help the wine keep its color when exposed to light and air later.

Step 5: Heat the water

When the water is about to boil, pour it in the container with the juice. Hot water is used because it kills most of the bacteria and yeast in the juice and pulp. If you don't do this, the yeast you will add to the juice later will find it hard to do its job because it will have to compete with this natural yeast present.

Step 6: Add the acid blend

This is a powder combination of natural acids—citric acid from citrus fruits, tartaric acid from grapes and malic acid from apples. If you cannot find this acid blend, you can use the juice from one lemon, but in this case your wine will be more prone to oxidation. However, it is always better to use either an acid blend or lemon juice than to use nothing, because your wine will be insipid without these acids.

Step 7: Add sugar

Add about two thirds of the sugar your recipe calls for. Give the solution a nice stir to help the sugar dissolve. At this point the solution is in the big primary fermentation container. Now you have to leave the solution to cool to room temperature. Before that, cover the can or container with a towel and leave it. It will take about ten hours to cool.

Step 8: Check the gravity

Check the gravity of your wine using a hydrometer. Add a little sugar, stir well and then check the gravity again. You should stop adding sugar when the gravity reaches 1.095. That's about 14% of alcohol. If you go over this point, you can add water to reduce the gravity to the desired level.

Step 9: Add the yeast

Sprinkle the yeast over the solution but do not stir. Some of the yeast will float whereas some will go to the bottom. This solution is now called the must.

Step 10: Attach airlock

After sprinkling the yeast, attach the airlock following the instruction for the type of airlock you have chosen.

Step 11: Fermentation

In about 12 hours, the process of fermentation will begin and you will see foam beginning to form. When fermentation has started, you should stir the solution twice a day. Use something made of wood for stirring. Do not use metal. You can also punch the bag with pulp a few times while stirring. Always keeps the container covered with a towel because it will keep out fruit flies and dust from your wine. Also check if the airlock is attached properly. You may want to have a spare airlock because foam created during fermentation may seep into the airlock. If this happens, remove the airlock, and attach the spare one, or clean and sanitize the airlock and replace it.

You should also check the gravity of the must once a day. While the yeast is reacting with the sugar, it produces alcohol and carbon dioxide. The produced carbon dioxide will leave the container but the alcohol will stay. So, the decrease in sugar means an increase in alcohol, so it means the gravity will drop. When the gravity reaches 1.030, you should siphon the wine into bottles.

From this point on, the yeast will produce less carbon dioxide, which means that oxygen will be able to reach the solution. For that reason, you have to protect it in closed bottles.

Step 12: Secondary fermentation preparations—clean the jugs

Prepare the one-gallon jugs. You should clean them thoroughly but do not use any soup because it will leave a film and you will not be able to rinse it. If you're using jugs that have already been used, and there are some deposits that you cannot clean, here's a trick. Put some gravel in the jug, shake it well and then rinse the jug with plenty of cold water.

Step 13: Remove the sack from the container

Squeeze the sack with the pulp until all the liquid has been extracted. Discard the pulp, clean and wash the bag with cold water, and dry it.

Step 14: Filling the jugs

Give the solution in the primary container a nice stir. Use a funnel and siphon to fill the jugs. Make sure that your siphon hose is clean. Place the container with wine on a table or chair and place an empty and clean jug beneath it. Dip one end of the siphon hose in the wine in the container. Then come close to the jug beneath and suck on the other end of the hose. You will feel that the wine is coming through the hose and when you feel that it is about to reach your mouth, place your thumb over the end of the hose to stop the wine from escaping. Now, place this end of the hose to the mouth of an empty jug, remove your thumb and start filling up the jug. If you are doing this for the first time, you may find it a bit difficult to do it all by yourself, because there are several things you need to pay attention to. So, you can find someone to help you until you get used to siphoning. Repeat the same process until you siphon all the wine into clean jugs.

Pay attention to fill the jugs only to their shoulders. The yeast can still produce foam so you should leave some space in the jugs. Attach an airlock to each jug. These are the secondary fermentation jugs. Place the jugs in a dark and cool place. The jugs should be covered so that light cannot reach the contents of the jugs. You can either place grocery bags over each jug or wrap the jugs with dark colored paper.

Immediately after filling the jugs, use plenty of water to rinse the primary fermentation container. If you leave this for later, you will find it hard to clean the residue left at the bottom of the container.

Step 15: Racking wine

When you notice that there is no foam on the surface of the jugs, you should know that this is a sign for you that you should siphon or rack the green wine into other clean containers. Also, run clean water through the siphon hose to make sure it is clean.

Siphon the wine following the same procedure as described in Step 14. Pay attention that your siphon hose does not touch the dregs at the bottom of the jugs. Since fermentation is over, fill these jugs almost up to their rims. Attach an airlock to each jug again. Repeat this process of racking the wine after three weeks and then at the end of three months. In case three months have passed and your wine is not clear, you cannot actually do anything except wait. The time different wines need to clear may vary and bear in mind that this haze you can sometimes see in wine does not change its flavor or taste, only its visual appearance.

Step 16: Bottling wine

To be sure that your wine is ready to be bottled, you have to use the hydrometer. It will tell you that the yeast will not react anymore. If the hydrometer reads below 1.000 S.G. it means that your wine can be bottled. Make sure that the bottles are thoroughly cleaned.

To fill the bottles, you can use the siphon tube again following the same procedure as described above. You can also buy a shutoff valve for this purpose. It allows you to stop the flow whenever you want.

For sealing your bottles, you can use either plastic caps or corks. However, it is better to seal them with corks, using a cork machine. The corks will need to be boiled first in order for them to be sterilized.

Step 17: Storing your wine

Now that you have your wine bottled, you need to keep the bottles in an upright position for about 3 days. Then, store the bottles on their sides to allow contact between the wine and cork. The cork will expand because of the moisture in the wine, creating a vacuum that will seal the wine properly. The bottles should also be kept in a place with stable temperature and with no light in order to allow the wine to age properly.

If your wine is stored properly, it should last for about 5 years, and quite possibly even much longer, before going bad. In case you open a bottle of wine but can't finish it, you can try putting the cork back in, though it might be a bit difficult. Also, keeping your opened bottle of wine in the fridge will slow down the process of your wine going bad.

Chapter 4: Red Wine Recipes

This chapter will give you a few red wine recipes that you can make at home. Since the whole step-by-step procedure has already been outlined, these recipes will include only general steps without any details previously mentioned.

MERLOT WINE

Yields 5 gallons

Ingredients:

70-75 lbs Fresh Merlot Grapes

3 tbs Oak-Mor Powder

3-3½ tsp Yeast Nutrient

¾ tsp Potassium Metabisulfite

4 tsp Pectic Enzyme

1 pkt Bordeaux Wine Yeast or 1 tube of White Labs WLP740 Merlot Red Wine Yeast

1 pkt Malo-Lactic Culture

Procedure:

Step 1: Destem the grapes and crush them.

Step 2: Use a wooden paddle to stir in ¼ teaspoon of potassium metabisulfite and 4 teaspoons of pectic enzyme.

Step 3: Cover the container with a towel and let it sit overnight.

Step 4: Add in the activated yeast, Oak-Mor and yeast nutrient and stir well. When primary fermentation starts, you will need to stir the wine twice a day.

Step 5: You will need to check for the presence of sulfur in your wine (use a testing kit and follow the instructions that go with it). When it reads below 15ppm, add the malo-lactic culture.

Step 6: When the gravity is 1.000, strain the juice and siphon it into the secondary fermentation container.

Step 7: Leave the wine for 1 month and then siphon it again to clean containers.

Step 8: Use a thin layer of chromatography assay (follow the instructions from the kit) to check malolactic fermentation (MLF). When completed, siphon the wine. Add ¼ teaspoon of potassium metabisulfite.

Step 9: Rack the wine again after one month.

Step 10: Repeat the procedure from Step 9 three more times. After the second and last racking, you will need to add ¼ teaspoon of potassium metabisulfite.

Step 11: Leave the wine for two more months.

Step 12: After this period, rack the wine again and add ¼ teaspoon of potassium metabisulfite.

Step 13: You can bottle the wine after 2-3 weeks. When bottled, keep the wine in a dark and cool place for half a year before tasting.

ZINFANDEL WINE

Yields 5 gallons

Ingredients:

60-75 lbs Fresh Zinfandel Grapes

1 pkt Bordeaux Wine Yeast

1 pkt Malo-Lactic Culture

3 tbs Oak-Mor Powder

3-3½ tsp Yeast Nutrient

¾ tsp Potassium Metabisulfite

4 tsp Pectic Enzyme

Procedure:

Step 1: Destem the grapes and crush them.

Step 2: Stir in ¼ teaspoon of potassium metabisulfite and 4 teaspoons of pectic enzyme.

Step 3: Cover the container with a towel and let it sit overnight.

Step 4: Check if sugar needs to be added. Add in the activated yeast, Oak-Mor and yeast nutrient and stir well. Stir the wine twice a day.

Step 5: You will need to check for the presence of sulfur in your wine (use a testing kit and follow the instructions that go with it). When it reads below 15ppm, add the malo-lactic culture.

Step 6: When the gravity is 1.000, strain the juice and siphon it into the secondary fermentation container.

Step 7: Rack the wine after a month.

Step 8: Use a thin layer of chromatography assay (follow the instructions from the kit) to check malolactic fermentation (MLF). When completed, siphon the wine. Add ¼ teaspoon of potassium metabisulfite.

Step 9: Rack the wine 3 or 4 more times. You should add ¼ teaspoon of potassium metabisulfiteat each time and siphoning should be a month apart.

Step 10: Bottle the wine when it clears.

Step 11: The wine should be left for half a year to age before drinking.

SYRAH WINE

Yields 5 gallons

Ingredients:

75 lbs Fresh Syrah Grapes

Gervin Varietal A or SB1 Bordeaux (dry) Wine Yeast

1 pkt Malo-Lactic Culture

3 tbs Oak Powder

3-4 tsp Yeast Nutrient

1¼ tsp Pectic Enzyme

Potassium Metabisulfite (as needed)

Procedure:

Step 1: Crush the grapes, stir in the pectic enzyme and leave to sit covered for about 4 hours.

Step 2: Add in ¼ teaspoon of potassium metabisulfite and leave to sit overnight.

Step 3: Take a sample of the juice and check if sugar need to be added.

Step 4: Add the oak powder and yeast nutrient. Stir well and add the activated yeast. Stir the must twice a day.

Step 5: On the fifth day of fermentation add the malo-lactic culture.

Step 6: Check the gravity. When it reads 1.000, press the grapes and return the juice to the primary fermentation container.

Step 6: When the malo-lactic fermentation is over, take a sample of the juice and stir in ¼ teaspoon of potassium metabisulfite. Pour this solution into a secondary fermentation container.

Step 7: Siphon the remaining wine into this secondary fermentation container.

Step 8: Rack the wine after six weeks and add ¼ teaspoon of potassium metabisulfite. Repeat this step until the wine clears.

Step 9: When the wine clears, leave it for 3 weeks before transferring to bottles.

Step 10: The wine should be left to age for at least a year before tasting.

Chapter 5: White Wine Recipes

In this chapter, you will discover how to prepare some well-known types of white wine, such as Chardonnay, Sauvignon Blanc Wine and Riesling Wine.

CHARDONNAY

Yields 5 gallons

Ingredients:

70 lbs Fresh Chardonnay Grapes

White Labs Chardonnay (Liquid) Wine Yeast

1 pkt Malo-Lactic Culture

3 tbs Oak Powder

2½-3 tsp Yeast Nutrient

1 tsp Pectic Enzyme

¼ tsp Potassium Metabisulfite

Procedure:

Step 1: Either destem the grapes or crush the whole cluster.

Step 2: Add in the pectic enzyme, stir well and leave covered for about 6 hours.

Step 3: Pour the juice in the primary fermentation container and place the pulp in a small mesh sack.

Step 4: Mix in the potassium metabisulfite and leave to sit covered for 6 more hours.

Step 5: If needed, adjust the sugar content and add the activate yeast, yeast nutrient and oak powder.

Step 6: Cover the container and keep in a cool place to ferment. The temperature should be about 650°F. Stir twice a day.

Step 7: On the fifth day, stir in the malo-lactic culture.

Step 8: Use a hydrometer to check the S.C. (specific gravity). When the hydrometer reads bellow 1.000, siphon the wine into the container for secondary fermentation.

Step 9: Keep the filled secondary fermentation jugs in a cool place where the temperature is about 55-60°F.

Step 10: After 6 weeks, rack the wine, add ¼ teaspoon of potassium metabisulfite and return to a cool place.

Step 11: Repeat the procedure from Step 10 every 6 weeks until the wine clears.

Step 12: When the wine clears, keep it in a cool place for 2 more weeks.

Step 13: Bottle the wine and leave to sit for 3 months before drinking.

SAUVIGNON BLANC WINE

Yields 5 gallons

Ingredients:

60-75 lbs Sauvignon Blanc Grapes

1 pkt Red Star Côtes des Blancs Wine Yeast

3-3½ tsp Yeast Nutrient

¾ tsp Potassium Metabisulfite

1/2 tsp Pectic Enzyme

Procedure:

Step 1: Destem the grapes and crush them.

Step 2: Stir in the pectic enzyme, cover the container and leave for 2 hours.

Step 3: Pour the juice into the primary fermentation container. Mix in ¼ teaspoon of potassium metabisulfite. Leave covered for 8 hours.

Step 4: Check the gravity and adjust the sugar content if needed.

Step 5: Add the yeast nutrient and activated yeast starter.

Step 6: When 12 hours have passed, stir the must well.

Step 7: Check the gravity and when it reads 1.000, siphon the wine to the secondary fermentation containers. Leave the containers in a cool place.

Step 8: After a period of a month or 45 days, rack the wine again and fine it with Bentonite. Leave for a month to clear.

Step 9: Rack the wine again, add ¼ teaspoon of potassium metabisulfite. Repeat the same procedure after a month.

Step 10: Keep the wine for 2 months in a cool place.

Step 11: Bottle the wine and leave for 3 months before drinking.

Conclusion

Yes, that's pretty much all you need to know to make your own wine. You probably couldn't imagine it being that easy. You just need the necessary equipment, which should not be at all something expensive. Then, you just need to follow the steps presented in Chapter 3, and be patient enough to wait for your wine to age and reward you with its wonderful taste. Cheers!

Finally, I'd like to thank you for purchasing this book! If you enjoyed it or found it helpful, I'd greatly appreciate it if you'd take a moment to leave a review on Amazon. Thank you!

Printed in Great Britain
by Amazon

57152486R00036